Paul Richardson

Railway Photographer of the Year 1982, 1983

The majesty of the steam train in colour

Osprey Colour Series

Published in 1985 by Osprey Publishing Limited
12–14 Long Acre, London WC2E 9LP
Member company of the George Philip Group

British Library Cataloguing in Publication Data
Richardson, Paul
   Evocative steam.—(Osprey colour series)
   1. Locomotives—Pictorial works
   I. Title
   625.2'61'0222   TJ605

ISBN 0-85045-654-1

Editor Tim Parker

Designed by Martin Richards

Printed in Hong Kong

INTRODUCTION

Railways up to the age of 13 years were just an aspect of transport or history. Stephenson, *Mallard* and other names did nothing except draw silent murmurs. Increasingly my school was swiftly overtaken by train-spotting and I was duly persuaded to be at Nelson station at some early hour of a Saturday morning for a day at Preston mainline station. Weeks passed and other more distant destinations, names and numbers amassed, I persuaded my parents to buy Ian Allan's *ABC* combined volume to record 'cops' (sightings) in ritualistic red ink.

A couple of years on I joined the company of a dedicated group of rail-fans of all ages who were superbly organized. We travelled the country often through week-ends armed with official visitors permits touring between 20 and 30 locomotive depots plus the occasional workshop. These calls were carried out with precision and no time wasted, sandwiches and bars of chocolate eaten on the road fenced off hunger but not so the consequential after-effects of bloodshot eyes, aching feet and often a grey facial coating of smoke and grime (or in today's terms, Shedbash Syndrome!) My constant companion, a battered *ABC* with over 11,000 underlinings is testimony to those memorable days.

Years on and with the radical transfor-mation of BR, interest faded eventually eclipsed by sport. I joined a cycling club with a strong racing squad and ten of my years were absorbed in competition, racing against the clock. Coincidentally I felt the need to buy a camera to record my fellow competitors to serve as a lasting visual reminder, and it was during my last season of racing, 'photography' became a new challenge. Learning to recognize potential subjects to fit into that rectangular form to become a picture became a passion.

Then quite by accident I became re-acquainted with a dedicated steam enthusiast and was urged to visit the nearby Keighley & Worth Valley Railway plus a chance to see *Flying Scotsman* on the mainline. In this brief encounter the fusing of railways and photography became absolute. The circle now complete, my adventure was starting . . .

Barriers were there to be overcome. Choosing locations to take the best advantages of wind direction, lighting conditions, locomotive characteristics was Lord. With each sighting, experience accumulated for use in the future. Self control was a vital quality for an approaching train can increase the pulse-rate causing unsteadiness. Living only 11 miles from the KWVR it can be considered my local line and therefore this book contains numerous scenes from this society's workings, the remainder being largely from northern England.

Constantly visiting the KWVR has helped me to appreciate this line with its continual climb to Oxenhope. Mixtures of curves, straights, gradients and line-side items of interest, the steep valley's slopes generate an evocative atmosphere. Frequently calling at Haworth Yard has enabled me to see locos dismantled, old paint, rust banished, parts replaced as required to be eventually re-assembled, painted and burnished to a gleaming example of preservation. Tremendous obstacles are cleared to return to steam. If it were not for highly motivated people since the end of steam on British Railways in 1968, almost all would have been lost to the torch.

When I photographed *Green Arrow* climbing past Selside my equipment was a camera body and just two lenses, but now I have four bodies and 12 lenses. A heavy tripod and all these are critically aimed to make pleasing visual statements, but the drawback of all this equipment is weight and when it becomes a burden I am sure I will be forced to return to the basics of Selside in 1978.

On accumulating lenses I first believed the only way to photograph railways was via long telephotos, my 'standard' was for many years a 200 mm. Its four-time magnification captures dynamism, pace and romanticism, but in retrospect other options appeared due to my changing ideas and I find myself using any lens from 35 mm up to 300 mm. In essence the viewpoint chosen dictates choice of focal length.

The choice of photographs for reproduction I left to my editor Tim Parker and Osprey's designer. Selecting the merits of Britain's variable weather conditions, sharp, clear pictures are not always a pre-requisite. A completely revealing truism, a low light and alluring atmospheric softness often illustrate a feeling of intensity appropriate to the steam engine's dominant years. The range of light and the degrees of sharpness present an ever-changing challenge to the steam railway photographer.

Finally I would like to thank and praise the many unsung volunteers and staff of the Keighley & Worth Valley Railway for the years of work keeping the wheels turning. Also all concerned with the Steam Locomotive Operators Association and other related concerns everywhere, and to British Rail in responding to the demand to help perpetuate the steam locomotive and allow it to perform duties for which it was designed and built for.

Paul Richardson
Nelson, Lancashire
April 1985

The sun partly filtered by thin cloud tinges
reflective surfaces as ex-MSC no. 31 *Hamburg*
draws away from Oxenhope with the shuttle
service for Haworth. 85 mm

Above
On loan from the NELPG, on this early morning enthusiast's day chilled by overnight frost, KI no. 2005 arrives at Keighley with a goods train prior to its 0830 departure. 50 mm

Left
On a late summer's evening with careful choice of angle to maximize on the golden sunlight reflecting onto LNER A3 no. 4472 *Flying Scotsman* heading *The White Rose* away from Bell Busk destined for Carnforth. 200 mm

Exploding from Shotlock Tunnel, revered LMS *Jubilee* no. 5690 heads the *Leander Enterprise* north. The journey south was to take place on the same day, a rare occasion for a Settle–Carlisle working. 200 mm

Racing up the gradient towards Clapham
station SR no. 850 *Lord Nelson* displays its
authority with the Cumbrian *Mountain Express*
bound for Hellifield. 200 mm

Right
The conditions are ideal, a following wind pushing to the right chases LMS no. 4767 *George Stephenson* which charges the bank from Settle Junction with a CME. 200 mm . . .

Below
December, the month when Santa trains are operated by the KWVR. LMS 8F no. 8431 leads an RSH 0-6-0 ST, the damp rails caused by this dense mist demand skilful handling by the footplate crews who achieve grip pulling out of Damems Loop, KWVR. 200 mm

. . . and in sequence 4767 emits this superb
manifestation of smoke and steam. 200 mm

The quiet of these woods is hardly interrupted
as no. 31 *Hamburg* trundles downline to
Haworth as it gives a branch-line atmosphere
on this January afternoon. 35 mm

Right
Leaving Chester still further behind, the resonant exhausts
deepen as the Inter-City double-headed by GWR no. 4930
Hagley Hall and LMS no. 5000 hug the rising curve at Radnel,
speeding onto Shrewsbury. 300 mm

Below
This group of early leafing trees is caught by a burst of
sunlight as paired saddletanks RSH no. 63 and Lancashire and
Yorkshire no. 752 pull away from Haworth. 85 mm

Overnight snowfalls have carpeted the land
creating havoc for road-users, hence only a
handful of photographers were able to witness
LMS Black Five no. 4767 *George Stephenson*
bring the southbound CME nearer to the
summit of Ais Gill. 105 mm

Re-opening the way for steam on the
Settle–Carlisle line Gresley's V2 no. 4771 *Green
Arrow* passes Selside as *The Norfolkman*
relentlessly attacks the arduous climb ravaged
by wind driven sleet. 135 mm

Above
Black Fives appreciated for their hard-firing,
seen here is no. 5305 which hauls a private
charter thus producing this sensational exhaust
screening off the Weeton Tunnel. 200 mm

Right
The signal drops and with the first beats of
exhaust BR Standard 4 no. 75078 restarts from
Damems Loop, KWVR. 200 mm

I don't often photograph steam in summer as the exhaust effects are usually just visible, but on this occasion I was pleased to capture no. 4472 *Flying Scotsman* storming up the 1-100 gradient at Mewith with *The Red Rose* for York. 200 mm

Obscured by its coaches RSH no. 63 pulls the
last train of the day from Keighley; calm
conditions allow the exhaust to climb desirably
upwards. 135 mm

Left
The sun breaks through scattered cloud to the timely appearance of LMS no. 5690 *Leander*, which powers round the curve near Coniston with the Trans-Pennine Pullman westbound for Carnforth. 135 mm

Below
With three coaches, ex-MSC no. 31 *Hamburg* nears Oxenhope, tints of reddish brown offer extreme surroundings to its past days on the Manchester Ship Canal. 31's centre driving wheels are flangeless, a specification required to negotiate tight radius curves. 200 mm

The essence of railways. People actively doing all manner of duties; here the unglamorous task of cleaning out the ash-pit at Haworth Yard help perpetuate the cause. 105 mm

Also civil engineering taking place as defective rivets are cut from this bridge section, 41241 and 34092 lay in various stages of restoration, Haworth Yard. 220 mm

On a sunny bank holiday Saturday morning at Steamtown, Carnforth, three locomotives raise steam for a CMP, SR no. 34092 *City of Wells*, LMS pair no. 5407 and no. 5690 *Leander* are each in turn given a thorough safety check by the BR locomotive inspector with his torch and long-shaft wheel-tapper's hammer. 50 mm

Mist and steam help define the shape of this
Santa Special, LMS no. 8431 and an RSH 0-6-0
ST synchronize effort approaching Oakworth on
this December eve. 200 mm

Getting into stride Jubilee no. 5690 *Leander* puts
in tremendous effort heading the Santa Steam
Pullman away from Carnforth to travel the
Cumbrian coast in relentless drizzle, which
though unseasonal, amplifies this vaporous
atmospheric scene. 200 mm

Above
Many hands set-to preparing Coronation Class no. 46229
Duchess of Hamilton, this the largest and most powerful
passenger steam locomotive class built for British metals, now
a jewel in the treasures of preservation, is brought to readiness
to perform the Carnforth–Leeds section of the Trans-Pennine
Pullman. 85 mm

Right
Designed for high speeds the greyhound-like shape of class A4
no. 4498 *Sir Nigel Gresley* simmers sets imposingly at Steamtown
front-end artistry compliments the SSS diagram. 200 mm

Temperature at freezing and RSH no 63 with
snow-capped coach nears Oxenhope working
the shuttle-service, KWVR. 50 mm

The rare appearance of a Royal Scot with its unmistakeable smoke-deflectors; sole example for mainline use no. 6115 *Scot's Guardsman* in war-time black livery passes Sherburn heading the *Yorkshire Venturer*. 200 mm

HM the Queen declared a national holiday on
Prince Charles and Lady Diana's wedding day,
on this same day the BR Cumbrian Mountain
Express was hauled by SR no. 850 *Lord Nelson*
from Carlisle to Skipton with tributory
headboard *The Wedding Belle*, and seen here
Lord Nelson travels light-engine towards
Hellifield. 200 mm

A cheerless day, though ideal for atmospheric results, no. 31 *Hamburg* barks up the long straight and closes on this avenue of trees and telegraph poles. 300 mm

Above
Almost an hour overdue caused by a problematic water-pump
at Hellifield, the ideal duo of Midland Railway Compound no.
1000 and LMS no. 5690 *Leander* thrash up the climb to
Helwith Bridge in pursuit of reducing the loss. This Cumbrian
Mountain Pullman's first stop was to be Appleby. 85 mm

Left
Pristine turnout of both BR Standard 4 no. 75078 and Ivatt
Class 2 no. 41241 take the curve away from Ingrow, KWVR.
105 mm

The dream realized that of a Compound/Jubilee double headed over Ais Gill, drivers and firemen deliver this supreme 'clag' of heavy exhaust passing onto Ais Gill Viaduct. Passengers lean out of windows to hear that rare Midland whistle, myself amongst a line-out of cameramen respond with firing shutters and motor-drives. 135 mm

Left

This steam portrait, the faces of SR no. 34092 *City of Wells*
cools having worked a CMP the previous day whilst no. 31
Hamburg raises steam for the day's service, KWVR. 35 mm

Below Left

Restored at Steamtown, no. 850 *Lord Nelson*'s nameplate is
polished, final preparation for working the Lancastrian 2
Charter. *LN* is one of a few locomotives on loan from the
national collection entrusted to various railway centres,
Steamtown being host to 850. 135 mm

Below

Hurrying LNER A4 no. 4498 *Sir Nigel Gresley* approaches
Wrexham station in charge of The Western Jubilee bound for
Chester. 135 mm

Spring-time and caught backlit, 8F no. 8431
clanks up the line to Oxenhope writing its
signature in steam, KWVR. 135 mm

Low cloud and mist linger on the slopes of
Whernside as NB no. 673 *Maude* rolls off Ribble
Head Viaduct, giving a Victorian presence to
this one-off view. 300 mm

Having taken part in the Rocket 150
celebrations, North British 0-6-0 no. 673 *Maude*
climbs cautiously towards Helwith Bridge on its
wet journey back to Scotland

Quaint, the dwarfish MSC tank has an easy day
with its only coach; no. 31 *Hamburg* below
Oxenhope. 200 mm

One of the National Railway Museum's
working exhibits, LNER V2 no. 4771 *Green
Arrow* bursts into view from Weeton Tunnel
hauling a British Rail Harrogate circular tour.
200 mm

Above
A beautiful sight of RSH no. 63, the only working steam loco
to be face-one leaving Oxenhope with the shuttle for Haworth.
105 mm

Above left
With the first strokes of the pistons no. 8431 blasts its
cylinders clear of condensation leaving Haworth Yard.
105 mm

Left
Now reaching fever-pitch, preparation began long before
daybreak on this enthusiasts' day morning, no. 63 and no.
752 are ready to be despatched for their rostered turns. 50 mm

Above
Acquiring a set of Pullman coaches, SLOA's titled headboard
was re-named. No. 4472 *Flying Scotsman* carries forward the
first Cumbrian Mountain Pullman towards Clapham. 135 mm

Right
Viewed from inside Mytholmes Tunnel, the ideal engine no. 63
leads K1 no. 2005 about to enter this black frame of shadow
on this enthusiasts' day. 105 mm

The journey began at Middlesborough, but now here on the S & C line Peppercorns Class K1 no. 2005 storms the climb at New Biggin with the Northumbrian Pullman steam hauled to Skipton. 200 mm

New territory for a West Country as no. 34092
City of Wells having been signal-checked at
Horton-in-Ribblesdale demonstrates its pace
gathering capability taking a CMP north.
105 mm

Magnificent demonstration of steam-power in
arctic temperatures, no. 34092 *City of Wells*
charges round the curve towards Kettlesbeck
Bridge with the Golden Arrow Pullman.
300 mm

Above
Battling B1 no. 1306 *Mayflower* storms towards
Silverdale with the Humber Venturer, the B1 is
at present on the Great Central Railway,
Loughborough. 200 mm

Left
With a backdrop of the Fells at Garsdale,
HLPG's Class 5 no. 5305 gathers momentum
over Dandrymire Viaduct on a northbound
Cumbrian Mountain Express. 200 mm

The early morning light glints on the shape of
Carnforth's Black Five no. 5407 as it awaits the
CMP to arrive. 5407 is to work the
Carnforth–Hellifield section where no. 850 *Lord
Nelson* will take over to climb the Long Drag.
85 mm

The last Santa train of this day with about 30 minutes of daylight remaining. S160 no. 5820 and Standard 4 no. 75078 having set back to Damems crossing gates steams through the loop building to this fine crescendo. 105 mm

Regaining lost time, the Yorkshire Range
headed by LNER V2 no. 4771 *Green Arrow* on
the outskirts of Sherburn speeds towards York.
300 mm

With zestful pace and of the designers' name
A4 no. 4498 *Sir Nigel Gresley* ascends the Long
Drag at Selside with a northbound CME.
200 mm

Left
Sparkling snow covers land and roof, LT
pannier tank no. L89 delivers this crisp plume
of steam after departing from Haworth.
200 mm

Below
Receiving attention ex-Longmoor Military
Railway no. 118 *Brussels* in snow covered
Haworth Yard. Brazier burns to console
numbing fingers. 200 mm

The shadow of a passing cloud fails to engulf
no. 5820 *Big Jim* climbing towards Damems
station, KWVR. 105 mm

A feeling of great anticipation; this golden
moment as SR no. 850 *Lord Nelson* accelerates
off Dandrymire Viaduct with this CME. 200 mm

Aiming to secure a reputation LMS no. 46229
Duchess of Hamilton hauling its extra long train
pounds over Lunds Viaduct with this CMP.
Wind driven rain presents a threat of slipping
but the *Duchess* held firm. 135 mm

With a commanding force of 40,000 lb tractive effort available, Staniers class 8P no. 46229 *Duchess of Hamilton*, with its four cylinders firing in pairs, tames Settle Bank at about 60 mph hauling this CMP loaded to 14 coaches. 105 mm

With the forced withdrawal from service of no. 63 which suffered over-heated bearings, the partly renovated MSC no. 31 *Hamburg* is pressed into service. It charges away from Haworth, cinders fly and at this work-rate *Hamburg* develops a resounding beat similar to *Jubilee*'s. 50 mm

Staniers 5 × P shows its worth attacking the
gradient at Crosby Garret. No. 5690 heads
south with the Leander Enterprise. 200 mm

Above
The sedate pace is evident as LMS 4F no. 43924 travels light to the Oxenhope sidings to draw its coaches for the day's service.
85 mm

Left
Framed between factory chimneys no. 5820 *Big Jim* climbs away from Keighley splashed by sunlight. The tall chimney on the left has since been reduced in height, a measure I believe, effective to save insurance cost. 105 mm

The valley's greenery provides relief for this scene of L & Y no. 752 bustling towards Oxenhope with a special train, 752's age is similar to that of the focal length of the camera's lens! 105 mm

The residue of winter lingers on the fells. Black
Five no. 5407 brings southwards the first
Cumbrian Mountain Pullman, cutting through
the shadow of an untimely cloud. 35 mm

The rising curves leading to Kettlesbeck Bridge
are taken in majestic stride by LMS Class
Princess no. 6201 *Princess Elizabeth* on its long
journey to Hereford; the Red Rose is wholly
appropriate. 200 mm

Bleak conditions confront LNER no. 4472 *Flying
Scotsman*. It brings SLOA's private charter
cautiously nearer to the summit of Ais Gill.
105 mm

Right
Tremendous display of effort from Class USA
no. 72. Variable air currents create this unique
umbrella of steam above this oil-fired ex-dock
loco. 200 mm

Below
Chequered history. First built in America for
the WD, then sent to and used by the Polish
State Railways, and now at the Keighley &
Worth Valley Railway. No. 5820 in its WW2
livery for the film *Yanks*. 105 mm

Above
The winter retreats leaving flattened grasses adding a new colour to the land as no. 63 climbs towards Oxenhope and lends scale to the valley. 50 mm

Right
Framed by branches, no. 31 *Hamburg* adds grace and splendour to this winter image. 300 mm

Mid-week summer service at a time of Keighley's holiday period, here Bulleids Class WC no. 34092 *City of Wells* enters Damems Loops with rosebay willowherb in profusion add another red tone lacquered by the summery rain. 200 mm

Late in the month of August, the ideal after-glow of sunset tones the sky as BR 9F no. 92220 *Evening Star* crosses Kirkstall Viaduct, Leeds, hauling the Scarborough Spa Express to Harrogate and York. 105 mm

The town of Haworth glistens with light rainfall as BR Standard 4 no. 75078 leaves a gradually expanding trail of steam in the valley. 135 mm

Glorious sunlight bathes Jubilee no. 5690 *Leander* climbing towards Gargrave with the Leander Pullman 2, its eventual destination being Sellafield on the Cumbrian coast.
200 mm

Hard-pressed climbing Selside, Class 5 no. 5305 with a CME. The introduction of six trains over the Settle–Carlisle was to double, such was the demand. 200 mm

In charge of The North Yorkshireman; LMS no. 5407 speeds away from Bell Busk. This summer-time BR special ran mid-week from Carnforth to Keighley and return. 105 mm

Rostered to work the Steam Carol Service, BR
no. 75078 connected to the coaches, passes
steam into the heaters whilst no. 5820 moves
forward to take on water at Oxenhope station.
85 mm

In action, no. 4767 *George Stephenson* slices
through a cloud's shadow near Kettlesbeck
Bridge powering a CME east to Hellifield. On
the move this running gear is a geometric
marvel. 200 mm

In this nocturnal view of Gargrave station, the silence is broken by the delightful beat of A3 no. 4472 *Flying Scotsman* as it thunders through the night heading the Fylde Flyer chartered by civil servants. 35 mm

With a CME LNER no. 4472 *Flying Scotsman*
passes over the A684 at Garsdale. 135 mm

Below
An appreciation as to why this Black Five is named after its
working days with British Railways. No. 4767 is the sole loco
experimentally fitted with Stephenson's link motion. 105 mm

Above right
The outward bound leg of the Fylde Flyer angles into the
morning light. No. 4472 *Flying Scotsman* nears Kettlesbeck
Bridge. 85 mm

Right
At a casual pace no. 31 *Hamburg* travels light-engine to
Oxenhope on this New Year's Day. 50 mm

Some photographic ideas sometimes take years
to arrive at. The voluminous exhaust expands
and rises into perfect harmony with this dead
tree; *Hamburg* at its best. 85 mm

This bizarre combination of SR no. 34092 *City of Wells* assists L & Y no. 752. Both produce crisp white exhausts on this enthusiasts' day.
85 mm

Above
Lightweight Pacific on its probationary run. No. 34092 *City of Wells* climbs spiritedly towards Kettlesbeck Bridge with a CMP for Hellifield. 200 mm

Right
'Streak' is a term belonging to train-spotters in the days of British Railways and is applied to A4s. Here no. 4498 *Sir Nigel Gresley* races up Mewiths severe climb with The North Yorkshireman bound for Keighley. 300 mm

Rumbling off Mytholmes Viaduct 4F no. 43924
is opened-up on the rise to Mytholmes Tunnel.
85 mm

The climb to Ais Gill grows more distant as SR
Class King Arthur no. *777 Sir Lamiel* coasts
over Arten Gill Viaduct with a CMP. 105 mm

Travelling east to west LMS no. 5305 and no. 4767 George Stephenson hauling the Santa Steam Special near Gargrave bound for Carnforth and onto Sellafield. 200 mm

A large gap in the clouds above allows enough
light through to capture Derby 4 no. 43924 and
LMS 8F no. 8431 storming to Oakworth with
the Santa train. 50 mm

The shadow advances nearer as LMS no. 8431
with drain-cocks open blasts steam onto the
track leaving Haworth Loop. 200 mm

Above
The track and points have recently been re-organized and critically observed by a plate-layer American-built no. 5820 which creeps over points aiding the bedding-in of sleepers. The self-propelled Grafton steam crane is laid up after its stint of lifting. 35 mm

Above right
Raising steam at Carnforth no. 46229 *Duchess of Hamilton* is highly polished to work a T-PP. Just to the front rests Aspinalls 0-6-0 goods no. 1300, although passenger lining and Lancashire & Yorkshire have to be added. 85 mm

Right
Three locos well placed in Haworth Yard, bunker to bunker are MSC no. 31 *Hamburg* and RSH no. 63; to the right is the streamlined casing of *City of Wells*, KWVR. 50 mm

Left
Clear of the road-bridge at Keighley station no. 34092 *City of Wells* is in the act of running round its train. The Golden Arrow headboards and flags are to the memory of the West Country's designer O. V. Bulleid. 105 mm

Below
The LMS Class 5 no. 5407 travels light – returning to Steamtown having brought the CMP to Hellifield, where upon the *Duchess* passed over these gleaming rails at 60 mph. 200 mm

Bringing the CMP to the top of the climb at
Eldroth S & D 7F no. 13809 works hard before
descending down Giggleswick Bank. 200 mm

The last flickers of daylight catch onto LMS no.
5690 *Leander* powering the CMP round the
wide curve at Smardale near Kirkby Stephen.
300 mm

Above
Double-headed Black Fives, no. 5407 and no. 4767 *George Stephenson* demonstrate matched firing as they assail the gradient to Helwith Bridge with the CME. 300 mm

Right
The marvellous interplay of elements; LT pannier tank no. L89 hauls its three coaches to Oxenhope. This was my winning entry for the Eric Treacy Memorial Competition 1982, to hold the Kodak Trophy and title Railway Photographer of the Year. 135 mm. Title, Golden Incident

British Rail's Summertime CME LNER no. 4498
Sir Nigel Gresley hammers through the silvery
rain at Crosby Garret perhaps re-living its
express charges from its east coast fliers of
yesteryear. 300 mm

In full flight no. 4498 *Sir Nigel Gresley* produces
this magnificent exhaust, quite rare for this
most efficient locomotive. Clear blue skies
prevailed for this southbound CME, challenging
the grade at Crosby Garret. The tall mast-like
telegraph poles are no more to be seen.
200 mm

Right
Surrounded by the lazy atmosphere of a summer's evening in August, no. 5690 *Leander* slowly crosses Arnside Viaduct with the Cumbrian Coast Express, just 15 minutes from Carnforth. From here modern traction will whisk the train up the west coast main line. 200 mm

Below
Prepared at Carnforth the resplendent turn-out of LMS pair no. 5401 and no. 5690 *Leander* travel light-engine near Clapham station to work north a CMP from Hellifield. The rising peak of Ingleborough would be an impressive sight for passengers travelling up the west coast route. 50 mm

Left
The Trans-Pennine Pullman steam-hauled from Carnforth by
LNER K1 no. 2005 climbs away from Shipley for Leeds where
Leander was to cross the Pennines. The K1 returned to
Keighley for a month's stay on the KWVR. 200 mm

Below
The Standard 4 no. 75078 has been passing hot steam
through the coach's heaters. No. 5820 having just coupled is
about to draw the stock for the Santa Carol Service at
Oxenhope. 50 mm

Left
The new paint gleams on LMR no. 118 *Brussels*; this oil-fired
loco saw constant service throughout 1984 helping alleviate
fuel problems. 50 mm

Below
The Santa Carol Service departs from Keighley by BR no.
75078 and no. 5820 *Big Jim*. Stopping at each station to
Oxenhope, passengers sang carols to the sound of brass.
135 mm

Right
On the greyest of days, the signal is raised and SR no. 777 *Sir Lamiel* accelerates from Garsdale with a CMP. 105 mm

Below
Close-up of 8Fs Walchaerts valve gear; old and new oils give a feel of the workhorses of BR days. 105 mm

Getting over the shock of riding onto the
metals of the Long Drag, no. 34092 *City of
Wells* speeds the CMP towards Settle station.
105 mm

A late summer's afternoon and Ivatt Class 2
no. 41241 climbs away from Haworth, KWVR.
135 mm

Travelling at rooftop height, no. 46229 *Duchess of Hamilton* thunders past Settle with a CME.
200 mm

Frost is in the air as light-engines LMS no.
8431 and LMR no. 118 *Brussels* head for
Oxenhope for the Santa service. *Brussels* was to
be the banking loco. 135 mm

Climbing hard on Giggleswick Bank is Black Five *George Stephenson* reliveried in lined mixed traffic black with no. 44767 on the cabside and British Railways on the tender. 85 mm

EPILOGUE

This is to say a warm thank you and hope that you have enjoyed these visual experiences as I have in photographing them. To those less fortunate in witnessing the sight and sound of steam, this selection of 1977–84 images will stir the inner sense; if any imperfections are evident in the text then you have my apologies and I ask you to accept that perhaps they are a weakness of being a photographer first and enthusiast second.

Paul Richardson
Railway Photographer of the Year 1982, 1983